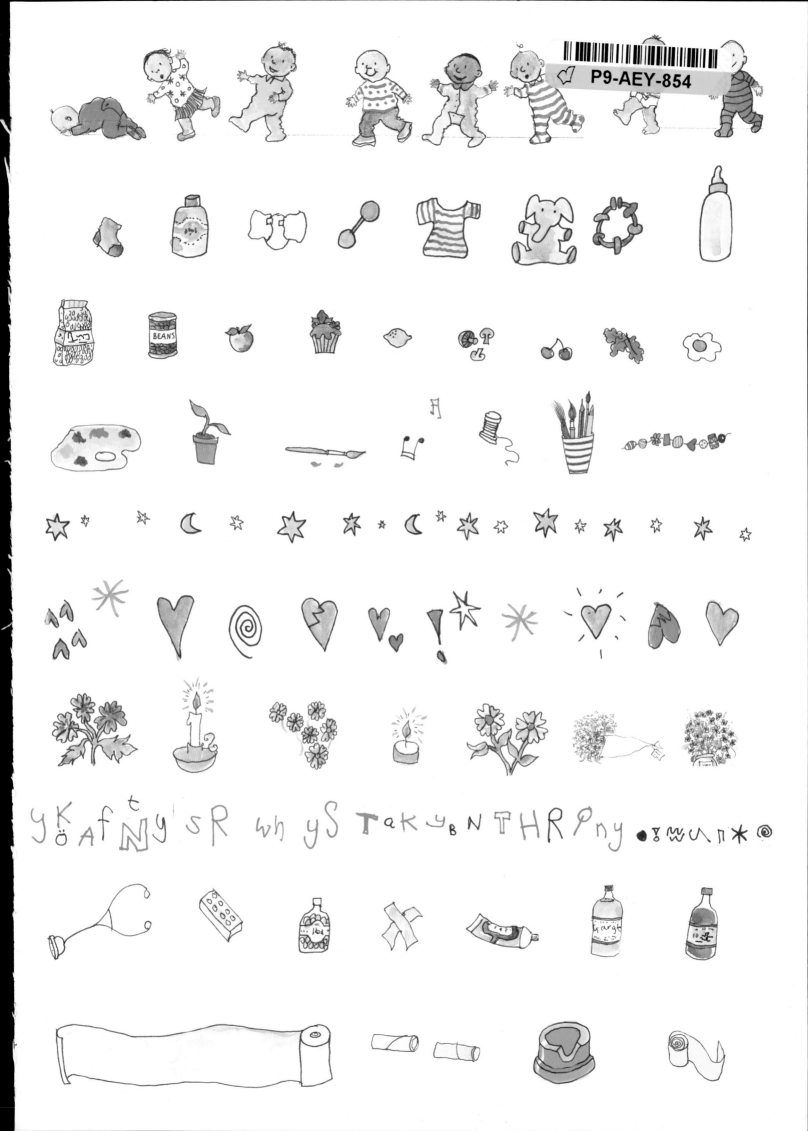

For Alice Biancardi —MH
To Theo and Olympia with love —RA

Inspiring | Educating | Creating | Entertaining

Brimming with creative inspiration, how-to projects, and useful
information to enrich your everyday life, Quarto Knows is a favorite
destination for those pursuing their interests and passions. Visit our
site and dig deeper with our books into your area of interest:
Quarto Creates, Quarto Cooks, Quarto Homes, Quarto Lives,
Quarto Drives, Quarto Explores, Quarto Gifts, or Quarto Kids.

Text © 2019 Mary Hoffman. Illustrations © 2019 Ros Asquith.

First published in 2019 by Lincoln Children's Books, an imprint of The Quarto Group,
The Old Brewery, 6 Blundell Street, London N7 9BH, United Kingdom.
T (0)20 7700 6700 F (0)20 7700 8066 www.QuartoKnows.com

The right of Ros Asquith to be identified as the illustrator and Mary Hoffman
to be identified as the author of this work has been asserted by them
in accordance with the Copyright, Designs and Patents Act, 1988 (United Kingdom).

A catalog record for this book is available from the British Library.

ISBN 978-1-78603-366-6

The illustrations were created with watercolors
Set in Green

Published by Rachel Williams
Designed by Judith Escreet
Edited by Kate Davies
Production by Kate O'Riordan and Jenny Cundill

Manufactured in Dongguan, China TL112018

1 3 5 7 9 8 6 4 2

MAY 2019

The Great Big Book of Life

Can you find ME every time you turn a page?

Mary Hoffman and Ros Asquith

Lincoln
Children's Books

HOW it all BEGAN

Aren't human beings amazing!
Look around you. Everything that has
been made—books, furniture, buildings,
toys, trains, roads, bikes—comes from
the brain of a human like you.
Someone who started life
as a tiny dot.

We almost all start as a bundle
of cells inside a woman's body,
which grow when a male and female
cell come together. Sometimes the
cells are grown outside her body
and put back in to finish turning
into a baby.

Being a BABY

It takes about nine months for a baby
to be ready to come out into the world.

You can't remember being born, but
has someone you know had a baby?
Can you remember what it was like
when they were born?

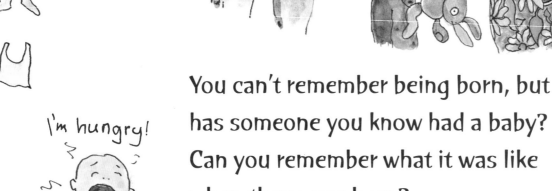

I'm hungry!

My bottom hurts.

I'm tired.

I'm wet!

I'm too hot.

Babies are so tiny and helpless they can't do anything for themselves except cry. It takes six weeks before they can even smile. And they certainly can't use words. So crying means everything.

I have to support his head, because he can't.

Six weeks old. Time to SMILE!

If human babies waited till they could talk and walk before they were born, they would be too big to fit in their mother's body or come out easily.

I'm cold.

My tummy hurts.

I'm angry.

I'm scared.

I'm lonely.

Babies may be helpless, but they are very good at CRYING!

But in the weeks and months that pass,
babies learn to recognize people and smile,
hold up their own heads, turn themselves over,
sit up, and then crawl.

They can clap their hands, blow bubbles,
chuckle with pleasure, frown, hold toys,
look at books, suck their thumbs, and twiddle
their hair. Soon they learn to pull themselves
up by holding on to furniture.

And once they can walk, they are toddlers.

Whoops!

Shhh, you'll wake the baby.

If you know any babies, you will see they sleep a lot during the day. But the funny thing is—they don't sleep so well at night!

For at least the first six weeks, parents don't get much sleep either, as someone has to get up and feed the baby a couple of times in the night. That's because babies' tummies are so small they can't drink enough milk to last them till morning.

Granny says it's good for babies to sleep through noise.

LATER...

Shhh! You'll wake the baby!

Some babies take years to learn to sleep through the night—those are the ones with the really tired-looking parents.

Everyone needs a good night's sleep throughout their life to refresh their bodies and brains. If we don't get it, we can be miserable and in a bad mood all the next day.

Is she getting enough sleep?

She is. But I'm not.

Guess who had a good night's sleep?

Eating & Drinking

For about six months, milk is all babies need to eat.

Then they start trying out new foods and making a big mess. It takes time to learn to use a spoon and put the food in the right place.

We should never have dressed her as a princess. All she'll eat is strawberries and cream.

Some babies eat anything and others are really fussy. Just like grown-ups. We all have favorite foods and things we really don't like.

But we all need lots of different kinds of foods to keep us healthy and give us energy.

CATTO NOSH

HEALTHY FOOD

NUTS

FRUIT

VEgeTables

FISH

I think I'll stick with MILK for now.

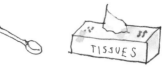

New babies get colds very easily because their bodies haven't met diseases before and can't fight them off.

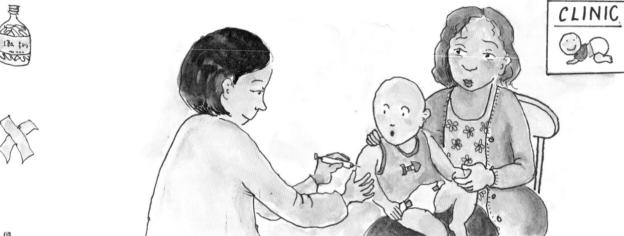

When babies are small, they are given injections called "vaccinations." They start getting their shots at a few months old. Measles, mumps, rubella, and chickenpox used to be called "childhood illnesses" but are less common now that babies are vaccinated.

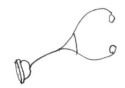

Other illnesses, like TB, smallpox, and polio are very rare now in countries where you can get vaccinations.

You don't need a doctor. You've just got a nasty COLD.

NASTY cold

NICE cold

Can flies catch GERMS? Do Mosquitoes get MALARIA? Do polar bears catch COLDS? Can SNAKES be POISONED?

If you do get sick, you can go to the doctor. But for some illnesses, there is no shot and you can get things like colds throughout your life.

A-tishoo!   Use a TISSUE!

At the BOTTOM

Between the ages of about two and three, little children start being able to control where and when they pee and poop.

So their parents get them a potty or a smaller toilet seat. This doesn't always go smoothly, and small people can have accidents or wet their beds for many years. But most people get there in the end.

Some things our bodies do, like farts and sneezes, are much more difficult to control!

LOOK who's TALKING!

When babies start to talk, they babble all sorts of sounds. Then they learn which sounds have meaning in their language. They start with one word at a time, and soon start combining them into longer phrases.

Little children say funny things sometimes while they are learning to talk and invent words and names for their toys.

The younger you are, the easier it is to learn a second language. Some grown-ups find it hard. But in many homes families use more than one language.

Talking is only one part of language. We listen and read and write too.

There are just 26 letters in the English alphabet, but we can mix them up to make thousands of words. It's strange to think that all poems and songs and books and plays and films are made up of so few letters.

What clever words you both make up.

No. I'm speaking Chinese and he's speaking Dutch!

We use sign language

Ooky

Pwaney waney

Is NOT pwaney, is AIRPIN

going to SCHOOL

Reading and writing become even more important
when we start school. Most people go to school
but some have lessons at home.

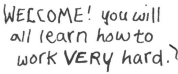

However you learn, it's important for the rest of your life. It helps you to get a job, and teaches you about the world and how to enjoy it. And it's where you make friends who may last for life.

School can seem as if it goes on forever—we start when we are four or five and leave when we are eighteen as quite different people.

But we are lucky if we have schools to go to. In many countries, children don't.

TEENAGE YEARS

Do you have a teenage brother or sister?
The teenage years of life can be very stormy.
From about the age of ten, your body can
start turning into a grown-up's before your
mind and your feelings have caught up.

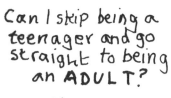

Teenagers can be moody and changeable—or
charming and helpful. Or both on the same day!

MY TeenAge SisTeR
in a BAD MooD.

My Teenage SisTeR
in a GOOD Mood.

They need a lot of sleep and get up late
in the morning. And they often like to
stay up late, listening to music and
playing games.

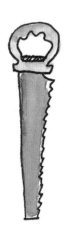

GOING to WORK

When we leave school, we might go to college
or start an apprenticeship. But sooner or later,
usually by the time we've stopped being teenagers,
we need to find a job.

Some people are lucky and find work doing something they love, at home or somewhere else. Others are not happy in their jobs.

And for many people it's hard to find any kind of work at all.

Grown-ups often find someone they want to go out with and maybe even spend the rest of their life with. This might happen when they are teenagers or when they are much older.

Some people have lots of girlfriends or boyfriends before they settle on just one. And some never do!

My 32nd boyfriend. He could be the ONE.

The only person who asked me to get married was my MUM.

But you don't have to have a partner to lead a happy life.

When two people decide to spend their lives together, they often want to have children. And so life starts all over again with babies!

But many people don't want to be parents and there are already so many people in the world that it's OK not to add any more.

Too many people. Too few CATS.

MIDDLE YEARS

When babies become teenagers, their parents are in the middle years of life.

All sorts of things happen to them. They may separate from each other and find new partners and start new families.

They may have great success at work or they may get into trouble with the law and have to spend time in prison away from their families.

They may change careers or lose their jobs and have to find other work.

They may enjoy many things outside work, like dancing, or playing sports or making beautiful things.

Or they might just like going out with friends or to concerts or plays or festivals or on exciting vacations.

My kids have left home, so I can do whatever I want.

I never had kids, so I've been doing that for ages.

OLD AGE

Teenagers grow up and leave home and maybe start their own families. So the people who used to be parents themselves become grandparents!

It's so much fun being a grandparent. It means having all the good times with the new children but still getting a good night's sleep!

As people get older, things may go
wrong in their bodies or their minds.
They may get sick or forget things.

Other older people stay fit and start new
careers or hobbies. As long as they feel
well, older people don't have to give up
work—especially if they do a job that
doesn't depend on being young.

DEATH

But in the end, all bodies wear out and people die.
It's just as well because if everyone lived forever
there would be no space in the world for the new
people being born.

STOPPED WORKING

Death is very mysterious and no one really
understands it. But it means that life has come
to an end. The person stops breathing and their
heart stops beating and the blood stops moving
around their body. So they can't
talk or feel or move anymore.
They have gone.

Have you ever had a pet who died?
Cats and dogs have much shorter
lives than we do, so we'll all know
something about death long before
we reach our own.

He used to
LOVE swimming
about.

Sadly, some people die before
they get old. They might have
an accident or an illness and
then they have a short life.
Others live to be really old—
over 100!

But we can remember people
long after they have died—the
kind of person they were and
what they did and said
in their life.

That's granny
when she was
your age.

BACK to the FUTURE

We may live on through our grandchildren, great-grandchildren, and ever so many descendants. Or we might be remembered for the things we did.

We all have a life worth living, whether we are rich or poor, famous or not, with a family or single.

Let's make the most of our lives and try to be happy and to make those around us happy too.

Life is for living—so enjoy every day!

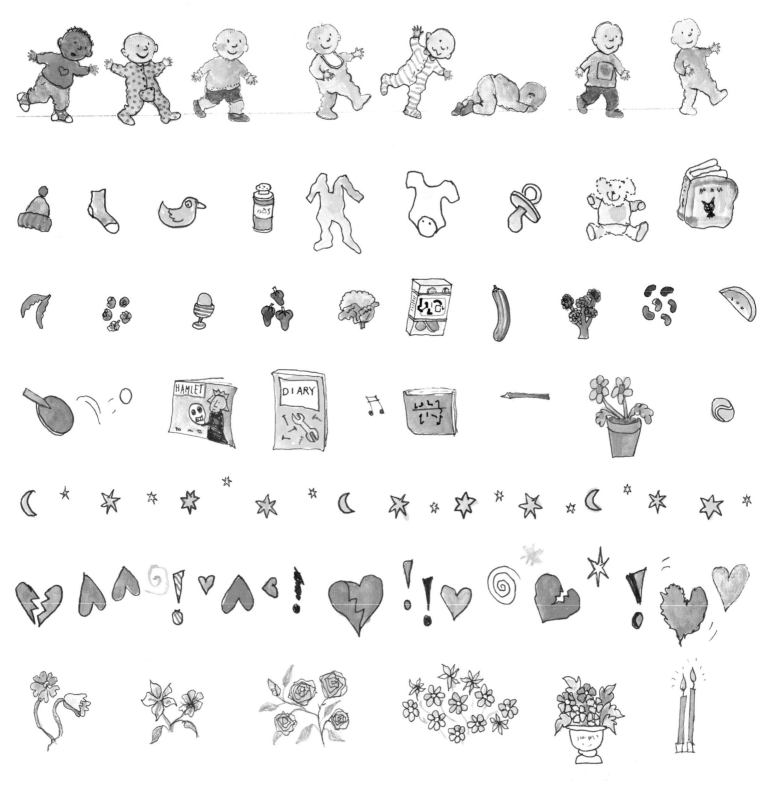